ANDY

An Alaskan Tale

Susan Welsh-Smith   illustrated by Rie Muñoz

CAMBRIDGE
UNIVERSITY PRESS

Words to do with Alaska

the Arctic – land north of the Arctic Circle

Elder – title of respect given to very old people

Kenai – the Kenai Peninsula in south central Alaska

ruff – a collar made from an animal skin (fox, wolf or wolverine), which is attached to the neck of a parka or the hood of a parka to keep your face warm when it is very cold

Inuit – person belonging to the Inupiat, the Northern Eskimo group

snow-go – a machine a bit like a motor scooter for travelling across snow

Published by the Press Syndicate of the University of Cambridge
The Pitt Building, Trumpington Street, Cambridge CB2 1RP
40 West 20th Street, New York, NY 10011-4211, USA
10 Stamford Road, Oakleigh, Melbourne 3166, Australia

© Cambridge University Press 1988

First published 1988
Fourth printing 1994

Printed in Hong Kong by Wing King Tong

Library of Congress cataloging-in-publication data
Welsh-Smith, Susan.
    Andy, an Alaskan tale.
    Summary: Relates the adventures of a sheepdog who comes
to live in a remote Eskimo village and how he and the native
inhabitants become accustomed to each other.
    1. Dogs—Juvenile fiction. 2. Eskimos—Juvenile fiction.
[1. Dogs—Fiction. 2. Eskimos—Fiction. 3. Alaska—Fiction]
I. Muñoz, Rie., ill. II. Title. PZ10.3.W487An 1988   [E]
88–10939

British Library cataloguing in publication data
Welsh-Smith, Susan
    Andy.
    1. English language. Readers – For children
I. Title   II, Muñoz, Rie
428.6

ISBN   0 521 35535 4   hardcover
ISBN   0 521 36754 9   paperback

About the Story

This story takes place in an Inuit village in Alaska in the Northwest Arctic. Although modern equipment is available, such as radios and snow-gos, the people still live in many ways a traditional life. As well as the snow-gos, there are still dog sleds drawn by huskies. And the Inuit are still very aware of the spirit world.

My husband and I both teach in a school in rural Alaska. Andy, an Old English Sheepdog, accompanied us to one of our village school assignments. The Inuit children had never seen a dog of that kind and were fascinated by him. They loved him. He shared our life for many years. Now he is dead but his spirit still makes us and the children smile.

I hope that through this story many children of different races and cultures round the world will come to know a special animal friend.

Susan Welsh-Smith
1987

For Hooter, Andy, Buffy and Ted – forever friends (S. & J.)
For Buddy-Pierre, this woman's best friend (R.M.)

This is the story of Andy, an Old English Sheepdog.

Not so long ago, this Andy came to our village.
He came on the Wednesday mail plane, along with
the packages and the green cloth mail bags.
Looking out through the window, with his
grey hair and whiskers, he looked
like an Elder!

We asked: "Who is this Andy? What is he?"
And everyone said, "We don't know."
This Andy is BIG!
We said, "Where are his eyes and tail?"
He has a lovely parka with a good ruff!

Andy has come to live with the teachers, and
we go to play with him at the teachers' house.

We brush his hair and make it full of curls.

Andy likes to play with us
in the school playground.
He can't sing like our huskies.
His song sounds like a cough!

This Andy likes to eat frozen fish, just like we do.

He likes to eat spaghetti
and meatballs, too.

When the snow comes, and covers the land,
it covers Andy too. He looks like a polar bear!

The teachers have a dog sled and they take Andy
for rides in it. He likes that!

Sometimes they go cross-country ski-ing
and get Andy to pull them along.
He doesn't like that very much.

One day, on a trip out to the hills,
he broke free and ran!

ANDY

ANDY

ANDY

ANDY

ANDY

All the white hills looked the same to Andy.
He was lost! He lay down and waited
to be rescued. The teachers were very worried,
so we all set out to look for him.
It was getting dark

and colder and colder . . .

Suddenly over the hill came Andy
riding on a snow-go!
The neighbours had found him.

One day the teachers moved to another village
and Andy went too. He was gentle
and kind to everyone, this Andy.
He had a good spirit and we liked him very much.
Even now he makes us smile.